Breakthroughs
IN SCIENCE AND TECHNOLOGY

Who Discovered
DNA?

Who Discovered DNA?

Jenny Vaughan

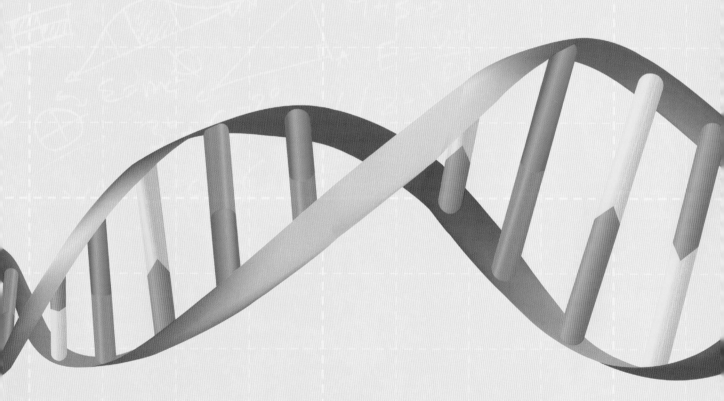

ARCTURUS

This edition first published in 2010 by Arcturus Publishing
Distributed by Black Rabbit Books
P.O. Box 3263
Mankato, Minnesota 56002

Printed in China

Planned and produced by Discovery Books Ltd.
www.discoverybooks.net
Managing editor: Laura Durman
Editors: Amy Bauman and Penny Worms
Consultant: Andrew Solway
Designer: Ian Winton
Illustrator: Stefan Chabluk

Library of Congress Cataloging-in-Publication Data

Vaughan, Jenny, 1947-
  Who discovered DNA? / Jenny Vaughan.
      p. cm. – (Breakthroughs in science and technology)
  Summary: "Looking at some of the major inventions and discoveries shaping our world today, Breakthroughs in Science profiles the research leading up to the discovery (not just profiles of the one or two key "players"). Each book describes the "famous" moment and then examines the continued evolution illustrating its impact today and for the future"– Provided by publisher.
  Includes index.
  ISBN 978-1-84837-679-3 (lib. bdg.)
  1. DNA–Juvenile literature. I. Title.
  QP624.V38 2011
  572.8'6–dc22
                              2010011021

Picture Credits
Corbis: cover (Dennis Scott), 8 (The Gallery Collection), 14 (Jeff Vanuga/Jeff Vanuga, Dubois, Wyoming), 36 (Jo Yong-Hak/Reuters), 40 (Amy Toensing/Sygma), 43 (Yonhap/epa). Getty Images: 31 (Science VU/Drs. H. Potter–D. Dressler), 34 (Sam Yeh/AFP). iStockphoto.com: 41 (Hans Laubel). Library of Congress: 29. Science Photo Library: 10 (Omikron), 17 top (JJP/Philippe Plailly/Eurelios), 18 (Dr. Jeremy Burgess), 21 (Kwangshin Kim), 23, 24 (A Barrington Brown), 28 (Ria Novosti), 39 (Corbin O'Grady Studio). Shutterstock Images: title page and 25 (Matthew Cole), 6 (Eric Gevaert), 7 (Alexander Raths), 9 (Geoffrey Kuchera), 12 (R Nagy), 19 (Michael Ledray), 22 (Damian Palus), 33 (Christophe Buquet), 32 (Pedro Salaverría), 35 (Henrik Larsson), 38 (Colette3). Wikimedia Commons: 13 (Linda Hall Library), 16.

Every attempt has been made to clear copyright. Should there be any inadvertent omission, please apply to the publisher for rectification.

The author would like to thank John Farndon for his invaluable help and advice in writing this book.

SL001445US   Supplier 03, Date 0510

Contents

The secret of heredity

An age-old mystery

What makes us the way we are? Why do some of us have dark hair and others have light hair? Why do cats only have kittens and never puppies?

For centuries, no one knew the answers to these questions. It took many years of inquiry and research to understand how organisms (living things) inherit characteristics from their parents.

Two kinds of study

Two different kinds of study led to this understanding. One involved breeding plants and animals and noticing how living things pass their characteristics, such as color, size, and shape, to their offspring. This is called **heredity**.

Another area of study looked at how organisms are constructed. Scientists learned that organisms are all made up of tiny "building blocks" called cells. The very smallest living things, such as **bacteria**, are made up of just one cell, while large organisms, such as humans, have trillions of cells.

THAT'S A FACT!

Some bacteria are so small that a million can cover the head of a pin.

Sheep, like other living things, produce offspring like themselves. The young inherit characteristics from their parents. In this case, young lambs, like adult sheep, will have four legs, will eat grass, and will have thick, woolly coats.

This photograph shows bacteria being grown in a laboratory. Bacteria are single-celled organisms that reproduce by dividing in two. They reproduce very quickly to make new organisms, like the original ones.

Eventually, scientists discovered that living things pass on their characteristics through something that is found in living cells. That "something" is an extraordinary substance called **deoxyribonucleic acid**, or DNA.

A great breakthrough

Discovering DNA and how it works was one of the greatest breakthroughs in

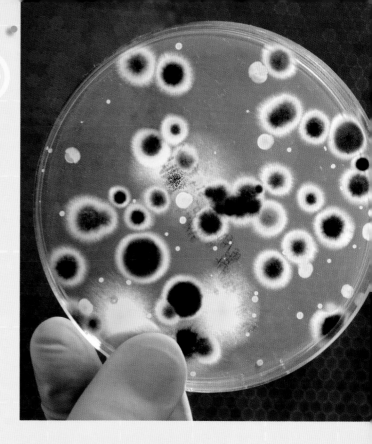

science in the last 100 years. Today, scientists know not only how DNA works but also how to use DNA to give living things characteristics they could never have naturally. They can even make clones— exact copies of organisms. They are now on the brink of actually creating life synthetically (from scratch) in a laboratory.

"I prefer to think that life comes from life, rather than from dust."
Louis Pasteur

Life needs life

Until as late as the 1800s, many scientists believed that some living things appeared "spontaneously"—that is, without any parents. For example, food that was left out would "spoil" when tiny germs (we now call them bacteria) appeared in it.

French biologist Louis Pasteur set out to show that even the tiniest life-forms had to come from somewhere. In a set of experiments, he boiled beef broth to kill any existing germs. Then he kept the broth in flasks with special filters to keep out any dust or particles. No germs grew in the broth. But when he opened the flasks to the air, the broth soon spoiled.

Pasteur's experiments showed that the bacteria did not appear spontaneously, but had been floating in the air.

Breakthrough

Louis Pasteur proved that life does not appear spontaneously. His experiments with bacteria showed that living things are produced only by other living things like themselves.

Heredity in practice

The first farmers

Even in ancient times, people discovered they could influence heredity. When early humans started to settle in one place, they began to grow the food they needed instead of hunting and foraging for it. These were the first farmers. Over many years, they turned wild grasses into cereal crops such as wheat, barley, rice, maize, millet, and sorghum. They did this in a process called **selective breeding**. They collected the seeds from the best plants of one generation of crops to produce the next generation of plants. Better, tastier vegetables were also produced this way.

Farmers realized that animals could be changed by selective breeding, too. They bred animals that had characteristics or **traits** they wanted, such as cattle with more meat and dogs that were easy to train for hunting or herding. But even though farmers had discovered that they could influence heredity, they did not understand what made this possible.

These pictures are from ancient Egypt, and date from around 4,000 years ago. They show us that people had by then already developed grain crops from grasses and bred farm animals from wild ones.

Old beliefs survive

For centuries, people knew from experience that living things produce others like themselves—that a human mother could not, for example, give birth to a rabbit. Yet not everyone was quite sure whether this was impossible—and they did believe that a mother's experiences affected the way her young looked.

For example, many people thought that if a baby was born with a cleft palate (a condition that affects the top lip; sometimes called a harelip) the mother must have come into contact with a hare while pregnant. Similar superstitions still survive all over the world.

About 12,000 years ago, people began to train wild wolves like this one, to help with hunting. Since then, they have used selective breeding to produce the different kinds of dogs we see today.

Breakthrough

People learned from experience that living things produce young like themselves. They learned to choose the best plants and animals to breed from. Over the years, they developed productive crops from wild plants and farm animals from wild creatures.

Building blocks

By the 17th century, both farmers and scientists knew they could influence heredity, but no one knew how it worked. To know how organisms "worked," scientists needed to find out what organisms are made from and how they are put together. This important step was made just under 350 years ago by an English scientist named Robert Hooke.

Hooke was born in 1635 and, as a young man, studied many different scientific subjects. He was a genius at making and using scientific instruments. One of these instruments was a microscope.

Cells

Hooke examined many different things through his microscope. In 1665 he published *Micrographia*, a book about the things he had seen. It contained one of his most famous drawings: an enlarged section of a piece of cork bark. The bark was made up of tiny sections that he called "cells," after the tiny cells that monks slept in.

*"It [was] all perforated and **porous**, much like a honeycomb . . . these **pores**, or cells . . . were indeed the first microscopical pores I ever saw, and perhaps, that were ever seen."*

Robert Hooke, from *Micrographia*, talking about his observations of cork bark.

Pictured below are the magnified cells of cork bark, drawn by the scientist Robert Hooke and first published in 1665. Hooke was the first person to coin the term "cells" for these tiny parts of living things.

What are cells?

We now know that cells are filled with a salty substance called **cytoplasm**, but they also contain tiny working parts, called "organelles." The most important of these organelles is the **nucleus**, which controls what the cell does. Most—but not all—of the DNA in a cell is in the nucleus. In order for an organism to grow, and repair any damage to itself, new cells must grow. New cells come from the division of old ones. Cells divide, making two new cells, almost identical to each other. This is called mitosis.

Cells reproduce by dividing, over and over again. Before a cell divides, everything inside it—including its central nucleus—is duplicated. The cell then gradually splits into two identical new cells.

Animal cells

The wall of a plant cell is made of a fairly thick membrane, or skin, so it is easy to see under a microscope. An animal cell is not so obvious. In the 1830s, German scientist Theodor Schwann was one of the first to see animal cells. In 1839 he and fellow scientist Matthias Schleiden published their theory that all living things are made of cells. They went on to find out more about what happens inside a cell.

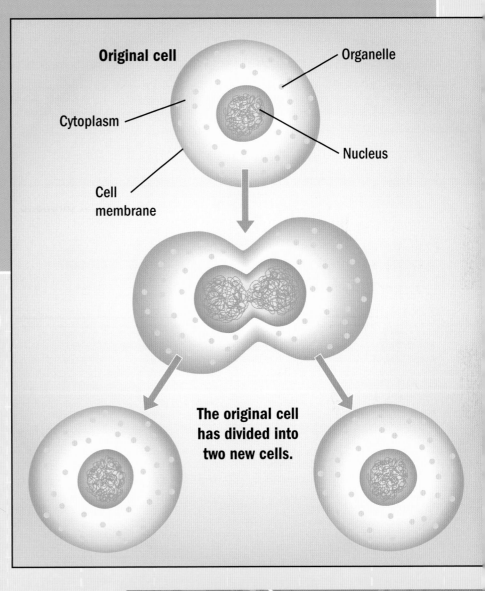

Original cell

Organelle

Cytoplasm

Nucleus

Cell membrane

The original cell has divided into two new cells.

Breakthrough

Robert Hooke made better microscopes than most of those made previously. Through them he saw parts of organisms too tiny to see before. He and others after him discovered that cells make up all living things. They are the basic building blocks of life.

Life changes

The story of evolution

Studying living things closely through a microscope is one way of learning about them. Looking at the way they live and behave is important, too. Charles Darwin was a **naturalist** who was interested in all aspects of the different varieties of animals and plants. In 1831, he embarked on what was to be a momentous journey to South America.

A journey of discovery

The five-year voyage on a British naval ship, the *Beagle*, eventually took Darwin around the world. He studied an amazing variety of creatures. He was particularly interested in those on the Pacific islands of the Galapagos. His experiences gave him the clues he needed for what was to be a groundbreaking theory. Darwin began to understand how living things change, or "evolve," over long periods of time, and how new species come into being.

Back home, Darwin continued his research by studying the way farmers and pigeon breeders used selective breeding to get the kinds of animals they wanted, by choosing characteristics they most valued. This led Darwin to conclude that selective breeding happened in nature, too.

Variation

The secret lay in what Darwin called "variation." This is the natural differences between individuals in a population (group) of living things of the same species, or type.

Charles Darwin

Date of birth: February 12, 1809

Place of birth: Shrewsbury, England

Greatest achievement: Developing the theory of evolution through natural selection.

Interesting fact: He almost didn't make the voyage on the *Beagle*— Darwin's father was not eager to let him go, but an uncle managed to change his father's mind.

Date of death: April 19, 1882

While visiting the Galapagos Islands, Darwin saw several types of finches, including this large ground finch. He noted that each had a different type of beak. Later scientists realized that the shapes of the finches' beaks had evolved to suit the food available on different islands.

Darwin suggested that "variations" can occur randomly. A variation that helps an organism survive in its natural environment will give it a better chance of living longer. A long life means it can produce plenty of offspring, which will inherit the variation. Other individuals of the same species may be born with other useful variations, and these, too, will be passed on.

Gradually, those organisms that are not so well adapted will die out, and their place will be taken by the better-adapted ones. We say the organism has evolved by a process called "**natural selection**," and new species have developed.

Darwin did not know what caused the variations or exactly how they were passed on from one generation to the next. But, over the next 100 years or so, the more that scientists discovered, the more support their findings gave to Darwin's theory.

". . . any variation . . . if it be . . . profitable to an individual of any species . . . will tend to the preservation of that individual and will generally be inherited by its offspring . . . [which] will also have a better chance of surviving . . ."
Charles Darwin in *The Origin of Species*.

Breakthrough

Darwin's greatest achievement was working out that evolution happens through the process of "natural selection." This theory is accepted to this day by all serious scientists.

Inherited "traits"

It was a long time before scientists worked out how heredity—on which Darwin's theory depends—actually happened. The first steps came through the work of an Austrian monk named Gregor Mendel. While tending his monastery garden, he observed the way plants inherited traits from parent plants. He published his findings in 1866. However, it was nearly another 50 years before scientists began to understand just how important Mendel's work had been.

Experiments with peas

One of Mendel's best-known experiments was with pea plants. Like many flowers, those of pea plants contain both male and female parts. The male parts produce pollen. The female parts, when **pollinated**, produce seeds (the peas in the pod). A typical experiment involved crossbreeding pea plants that always produced yellow peas with ones that always produced green peas. All the offspring produced only yellow peas—no green, or greeny yellow ones. They seemed to have inherited only yellowness.

Mendel planted these yellow peas, which grew into plants and produced flowers. He "self-pollinated" these (**fertilized** them with their own pollen). Amazingly, only three out of four of the resulting pea plants produced yellow peas. Roughly one plant in four produced green peas, though it had no "green" parents. It was as if the instruction to produce green peas had been hiding somewhere in the parent plant.

This albino (white) deer lacks normal coloring because it has inherited the recessive, defective gene that causes this from both its parents. Its parents were probably brown, but they both passed on the albino-causing gene. If only one parent had the recessive gene, the deer would have been brown.

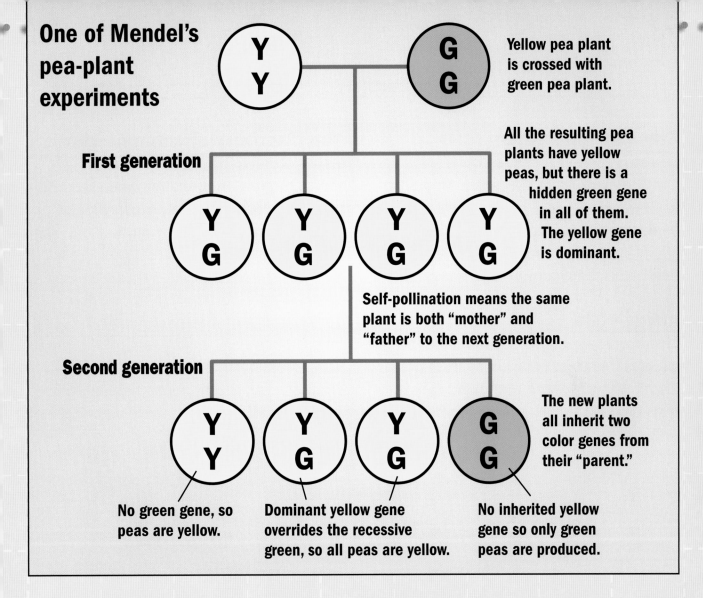

One of Mendel's pea-plant experiments

Yellow pea plant is crossed with green pea plant.

First generation

All the resulting pea plants have yellow peas, but there is a hidden green gene in all of them. The yellow gene is dominant.

Self-pollination means the same plant is both "mother" and "father" to the next generation.

Second generation

The new plants all inherit two color genes from their "parent."

No green gene, so peas are yellow.

Dominant yellow gene overrides the recessive green, so all peas are yellow.

No inherited yellow gene so only green peas are produced.

Conclusions

Mendel concluded that living things inherit traits (such as color) from their parents, and that:

1. Traits are passed from one generation to another and are carried by "factors" which we now call "**genes**."
2. We now know that individuals inherit one gene for each trait from each parent. A pea plant with one green parent and one yellow parent inherits one green and one yellow gene.
3. A trait can be passed on without showing up. Today, we know this is because genes can be "dominant" or "recessive." The recessive green pea gene only shows up when a plant inherits it from both parents, and there is no dominant yellow gene to "hide" it.

Breakthrough

Gregor Mendel discovered that certain traits are only seen if they are inherited from both parents. This led later scientists to understand how some genes (which carry the traits) are "dominant" and some "recessive."

Finding DNA and chromosomes

Clues to the mystery

The story of making sense of heredity is like finding clues to a mystery. Mendel's work was one clue. The next was the discovery of DNA, in 1869, by a Swiss chemist named Friedrich Miescher. After that came the discovery of **chromosomes**.

Inside cells

Miescher's research focused on the inside of cells. Rather gruesomely, he used **pus** and blood cells squeezed from bandages taken from a hospital. Later, he experimented with salmon sperm cells. He separated out the nucleus from the rest of the cell and did tests to find out what it was made of.

Miescher found the nucleus contained **protein** and another substance. This other substance was slightly acidic, so he called it **nucleic acid**. We now call it DNA. Miescher did not know it, but DNA is the substance that genes are made of.

The discovery of chromosomes

Scientists already knew that, for living things to grow and repair themselves, their cells must divide to make new cells. In 1882, German scientist Walther Flemming noticed tiny threadlike structures in cells that were about to divide. These threads were what we now call chromosomes. Each chromosome is one enormously long DNA "string," coiled up tightly around special proteins. Before a cell divides, it duplicates all its chromosomes, so that each new cell gets a complete set.

THAT'S A FACT!

DNA **molecules** are like strings. If all the strings of DNA in a single cell were uncoiled and placed end to end, they would be more than 6.6 feet (2 m) long.

Johann Friedrich Miescher

Date of birth: August 13, 1844

Place of birth: Basel, Switzerland

Greatest achievement: The discovery of DNA.

Interesting fact: Miescher wanted to be a doctor, but he was slightly deaf, so he decided to concentrate on science instead.

Date of death: August 26, 1895

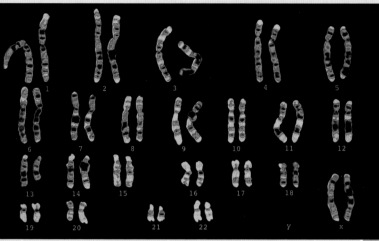

Chromosomes

All living things have chromosomes. Different living things have different numbers of them. Rice, for example has 12, but fruit flies have just four. Each chromosome is a single, enormously long DNA molecule. Along its length are many different genes.

Humans have 23 pairs of chromosomes (46 in total). In most pairs, the chromosomes are always the same size, but one pair is different. In a female, the two chromosomes in this pair—called X chromosomes—are alike. However, in males the pair do not match; there is one X chromosome and one, much smaller, Y chromosome.

In humans, and other life-forms that reproduce sexually, both the male sex cells (sperm or pollen) and the female sex cells (eggs) contain only one chromosome from each pair. When the sex cells combine to start a new life, the single chromosomes form pairs, with one chromosome from each parent.

There are 23 pairs of chromosomes in almost every human cell. These are a woman's chromosomes, with two X chromosomes. In a man, the chromosomes in the 23rd pair would be one X and one much smaller Y chromosome.

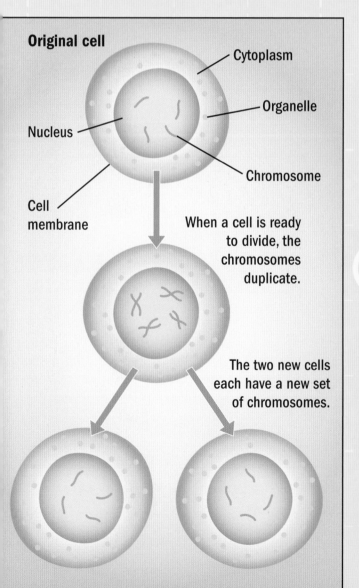

Original cell

Cytoplasm

Organelle

Nucleus

Chromosome

Cell membrane

When a cell is ready to divide, the chromosomes duplicate.

The two new cells each have a new set of chromosomes.

Before a cell divides, all the chromosomes inside it duplicate. That means that there is a full set of chromosomes in each new cell.

Breakthrough

Friedrich Miescher discovered DNA, though it was left to later scientists to learn the importance of this. Walther Flemming learned how chromosomes behave.

A smelly laboratory

So far, scientists knew what chromosomes looked like. But what did they do?

The answer came in a smelly laboratory, filled with overripe fruit, which attracted tiny fruit flies. The laboratory was set up in 1911, at Columbia University, New York, by Professor Thomas Hunt Morgan. Morgan studied **mutations** in the flies —which we now know are caused by changes to one small part of a living thing's DNA. Morgan used fruit flies because they reproduce quickly.

By this time, Mendel's work had been rediscovered. Scientists began using the word "gene" for Mendel's "factors," but they had not yet connected genes with DNA.

Looking at the eyes

One mutation that Morgan's team found was that some flies had white eyes instead of the normal red. Also, when a white-eyed fly mated with a red-eyed one, all the offspring had red eyes, although white eyes could then appear in the next generation.

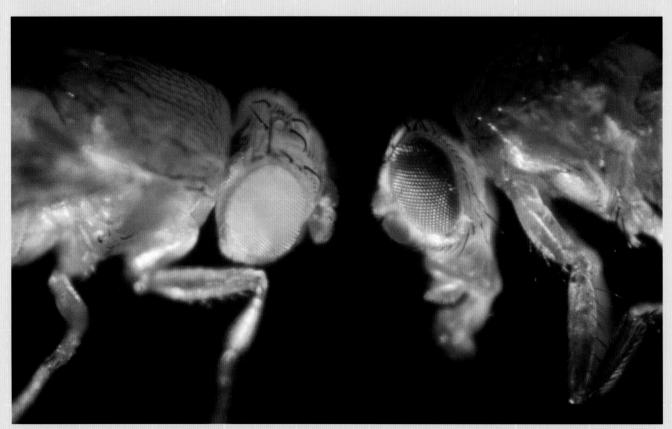

A magnified picture of two fruit flies, of the kind Professor Morgan studied. The white eyes were one of the first mutations that Morgan noticed; most fruit flies have red eyes.

Thomas Hunt Morgan

Date of birth: September 25, 1866

Place of birth: Lexington, Kentucky.

Greatest achievement: His work on chromosomes and heredity.

Interesting fact: His laboratory was messy, and he often left notes to his colleagues on scraps of paper covered with squashed flies.

Date of death: December 4, 1945

A link to chromosomes

Morgan noticed that the unusual white eyes normally showed up only among males. Why did males inherit these eyes, and not females? He knew that what made males and females different from each other was having slightly different chromosomes. So, he concluded, heredity (and genes) must be something to do with chromosomes. It was the first proof that heredity is linked to chromosomes. Some scientists had already suggested this, but Morgan had not believed it at first.

Morgan and, later, other scientists went on to find and breed from other mutant fruit flies—such as flies with differently colored bodies or differently sized wings. From these, they studied combined mutations (flies with more than one mutation).

Inheritance gets complicated

Studies of heredity done at this time revealed just how complicated it could be. The simple rules that Mendel had discovered did not always work. For example, snapdragon plants with red and white flowers can crossbreed to produce pink offspring. This is what is called "incomplete dominance," because the red gene only partly dominates.

A bed of red, white, and pink snapdragons. The genes passed between generations of the red and white flowers have become mixed to produce plants whose flowers are pink—a mix of white and red.

Breakthrough

Morgan finally proved that genes are carried on chromosomes and that they are the basic mechanism for passing on characteristics from generation to generation.

At last . . . the truth about DNA

Working with bacteria

During the 1920s, scientists started using bacteria to study genes. Because bacteria are single-celled organisms, they reproduce even faster than fruit flies, and in even larger numbers. As the story of DNA unfolded, bacteria began to play a large part in finding out more about heredity and how it happens.

"The transforming factor"

In the 1920s, British scientist Fred Griffith worked with a type of bacteria that had two forms. One was harmless, while the other caused pneumonia in mice. He found he could move material from the harmful kind into the harmless one, transforming it so that it became harmful, too. He realized that the material he had

moved must contain a "transforming factor." The transformed bacteria went on to reproduce as harmful bacteria, too—meaning the "factor" could be inherited.

Extra DNA

Most DNA lies in the chromosomes, within the nucleus of a cell. But there is also DNA outside the nucleus, in tiny organelles (working parts) called **mitochondria**. These use the nutrients from food to make the energy that cells need to reproduce and work. This DNA is called "mitochondrial DNA."

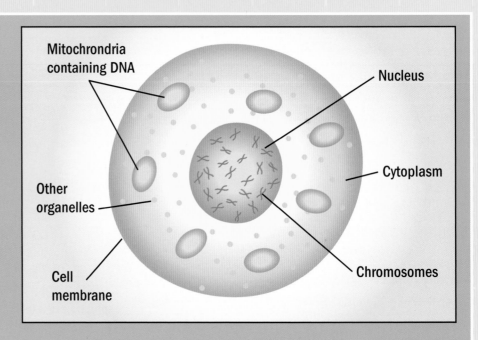

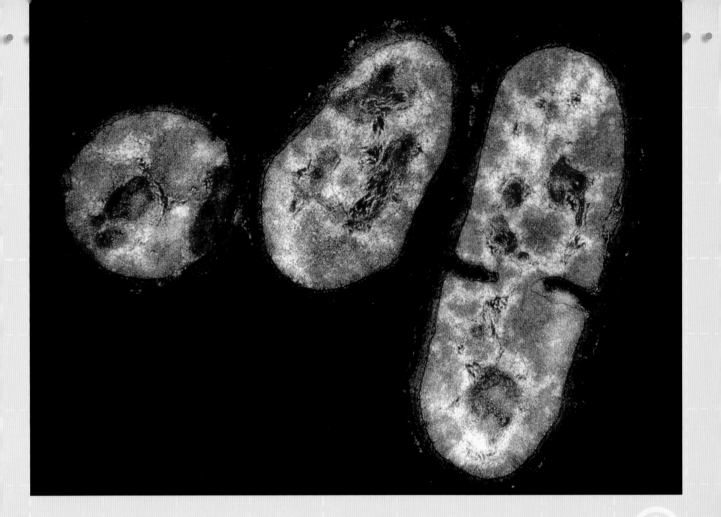

Finding the factor

In the 1940s, Canadian Oswald Avery did more experiments with pneumonia bacteria to try to find the transforming factor. In one experiment, he destroyed all the protein in the harmful bacteria. He found that they could still transform harmless bacteria. But when he used bacteria in which he had destroyed all the DNA, he found that they no longer turned harmless bacteria into harmful ones.

"... most people didn't take [Avery] seriously. Because you could always argue that his observations were limited to bacteria ..."
James Watson (see page 24) explaining the reason why Avery didn't win the Nobel Prize at the time of his discovery.

This is an image of the type of bacteria that causes acne, magnified almost 28,000 times. As single-celled organisms, bacteria reproduce by dividing, which they can do very fast. You can see the bacterium on the right is in the process of dividing into two cells.

He had shown that DNA was the genetic material—it carries the information that cells pass on to their descendants.

Breakthrough

Oswald Avery discovered that it is DNA that carries genetic information. This is passed on into new cells as organisms grow, reproduce, and repair themselves.

Finding out more

Now that scientists understood what DNA did, they began to find out more about it. They discovered what it is made from, what shape its molecules are, and finally, how it actually works.

Nitrogenous bases

Back in the 1920s, the Russian-born American scientist, Phoebus Levene had discovered that each molecule of DNA contains four nitrogenous bases (chemical units containing nitrogen). These are adenine (usually shortened to "A"), thymine (T), guanine (G), and cytosine (C). He also found that DNA contains sugar and a phosphate (material containing phosphorous).

In 1949, Austrian-born Erwin Chargaff continued Levene's work by studying the DNA in a range of different organisms, from simple bacteria to cattle. He discovered that, in every case, there was almost as much A as T and, similarly,

Erwin Chargaff tested the DNA in calves and a number of other living things. He found that the proportions of the bases adenine and thymine were about the same, as were those of guanine and cytosine.

almost the same amount of G as C. This suggested links between A and T, and G and C. But what these links were, remained to be discovered.

The clue to the shape

In 1953, the American biochemist Linus Pauling suggested that DNA was the shape of a triple spiral, with the phosphates on the inside and the bases on the outside. Little did he know, but a young English chemist named Rosalind Franklin, at King's College in London, was already on the way to proving him wrong. In 1952, she was working with X-ray crystallography (using X-rays to determine the shapes of molecules in crystals).

She produced many photographs of DNA molecules, one of which has since become world famous. Although she did not immediately see it herself, it showed that DNA does indeed have a spiral shape, but it is very different from the one Pauling suggested.

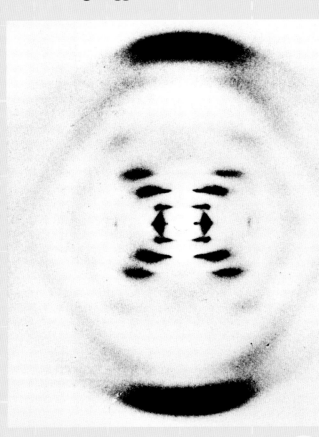

This photograph, taken by Rosalind Franklin in 1952, gave a clue to the shape of the DNA molecule. This provided the basis for the most important breakthrough in the study of the structure of DNA.

Rosalind Elsie Franklin

Date of birth: July 25, 1920

Place of birth: London, England

Greatest achievement: Using X-ray crystallography to produce a photograph that gave clues to the structure of DNA.

Interesting fact: After leaving college, she held a research post where her work became important in the development of carbon-fiber technology.

Date of death: April 16, 1958

Breakthrough

The work of Phoebus Levene and Erwin Chargaff determined that DNA molecules contain nitrogenous bases: A, T, G, and C, and that there are equal amounts of A and T, and of G and C. But it was a photograph taken by Rosalind Franklin that provided the vital clue to discovering the shape and structure of DNA.

Double twist

Franklin's photograph

In the early 1950s, scientists Francis Crick and James Watson were working at a laboratory in Cambridge, England. They wanted to find the structure of DNA. Their friend Maurice Wilkins showed them Rosalind Franklin's photograph. (He worked in the same laboratory as Franklin at King's College in London.) This provided Crick and Watson with the breakthrough they needed.

Putting the evidence together

Crucial clues in the photograph helped Crick and Watson to figure out that the DNA molecule is a "double **helix**"—a spiral with two strands, like a twisted ladder. The sides of the "ladder" are made up of groups of sugars and phosphates.

The bases (A, T, C, and G) stick out from the sides of the ladder at regular intervals. When bases from each side meet, they join, forming the ladder's "rungs." Bases can only pair in specific ways: A always pairs with T, and G pairs with C.

Reproducing DNA

It became clear that, before a cell divides, each DNA molecule copies itself, so that each new cell will have a full DNA "set."

How does this happen? First, the two DNA strands "unzip" from each other. Then a matching chain forms on each of the separated strands. The result is two new double-stranded molecules.

James Dewey Watson

Date of birth: April 6, 1928
Place of birth: Chicago, Illinois
Greatest achievement: With Francis Crick and Maurice Wilkins, he worked out the structure of DNA and how it reproduces.
Interesting fact: As a boy, Watson loved bird-watching, which led him to study zoology and then genetics.

Watson (left) and Francis Crick with their model of DNA.

This diagram shows the "double helix" shape of the DNA molecule. It is like a twisted ladder. Some rungs are made from the bases adenine (A) and thymine (T); others are made from guanine (G) and cytosine (C).

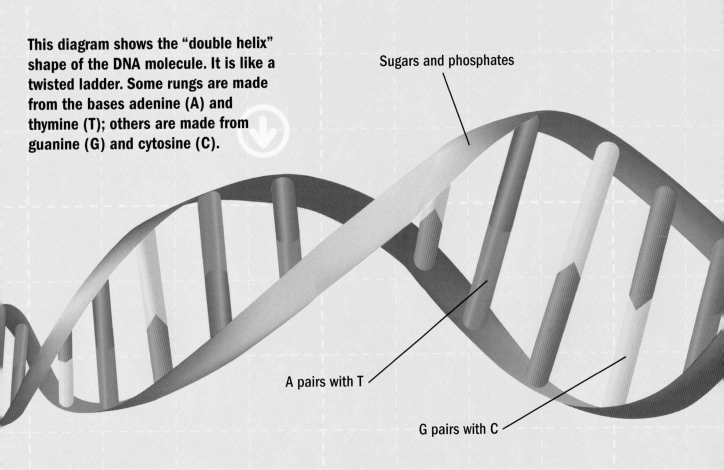

Sugars and phosphates

A pairs with T

G pairs with C

"We have found the secret of life."
Francis Crick and James Watson's announcement when they went to The Eagle pub in Cambridge, England, to celebrate the fact that they had worked out the structure of DNA.

Finding out that DNA could copy itself was an important discovery. It showed how DNA and the genetic information it carries can pass into new cells. This includes the sex cells that parents produce to make offspring. Because offspring inherit their parents' DNA, they are like them.

Crick and Watson, along with Maurice Wilkins, were awarded the 1962 Nobel Prize in Physiology or Medicine "for their discoveries concerning the molecular structure of nucleic acids and its significance for information transfer in living material." It is often suggested that Rosalind Franklin should have shared the prize for her work on DNA. But she died in 1958, and Nobel Prizes are only given to living people.

Breakthrough

Crick and Watson discovered the structure of DNA. From this they worked out how it is passed on as cells divide and form new cells. They had solved the age-old mystery of heredity, and this paved the way for huge scientific and medical advances.

The messenger and the code

Coded messages

The next question scientists needed to answer was, how does DNA pass on information to the cells, so that they know what to do?

Crick and his colleagues found that the order of bases along the DNA molecule is a code. This code is used to give the cell instructions for making proteins. Proteins are the substances that do all of the important work in cells.

DNA makes RNA makes proteins

DNA does not give its coded instructions directly to the cell. Instead, it passes them on through another nucleic acid, called ribonucleic acid (RNA). This allows the DNA to remain in the cell nucleus, safe from damage.

Sections of the DNA molecule are copied to RNA, which then becomes mRNA (messenger RNA). This carries the DNA "message" out of the nucleus. In the cytoplasm, mRNA is "translated" into proteins. This happens on tiny, rounded organelles called ribosomes.

The importance of proteins

Proteins do most of the really important jobs in living cells. Many parts of the cell are made from proteins. Proteins also control the thousands of chemical reactions that happen inside cells.

Each kind of protein is made from a long string of subunits, called **amino acids**. The amino acids have to be in exactly the right order along the protein chain. If not, the protein cannot do its job.

Making proteins

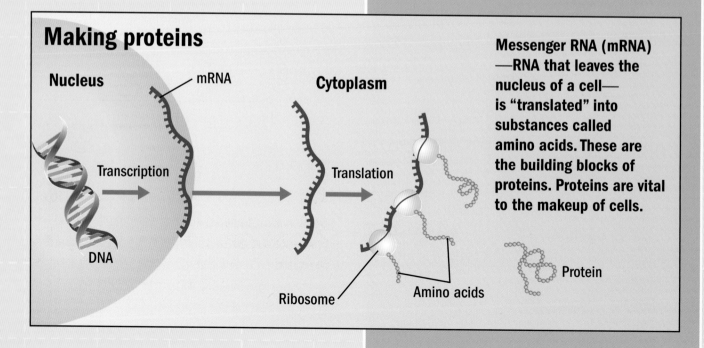

Nucleus

mRNA

Cytoplasm

Transcription

Translation

DNA

Ribosome

Amino acids

Protein

Messenger RNA (mRNA) —RNA that leaves the nucleus of a cell— is "translated" into substances called amino acids. These are the building blocks of proteins. Proteins are vital to the makeup of cells.

Francis Harry Compton Crick

Date of birth: June 8, 1916

Place of birth: Northampton, England

Greatest achievements: Understanding how DNA is constructed, how it carries information, and the role of RNA.

Interesting fact: During World War II, Francis Crick worked developing radar and magnetic mines for naval warfare.

Date of death: July 28, 2004

ribosome reads the bases AGG on the mRNA, it attaches arginine to the protein chain. Each triplet of bases on the RNA is translated into an animo acid, so that the protein chain is built in the right order.

The bases that line a strand of DNA form a kind of code. Each group of three bases gives instructions for making one amino acid.

The genetic code

DNA and RNA molecules are made up of just four different bases. However, there are 20 different amino acids. So, how could a four-letter "alphabet" produce a code for 20 different amino acids? This was a huge puzzle to scientists for many years. The answer is that each amino acid is coded by a "word" made up of three bases. For example, suppose the first three bases on a piece of mRNA are AGG. In genetic code, this is an amino acid called arginine. So when a

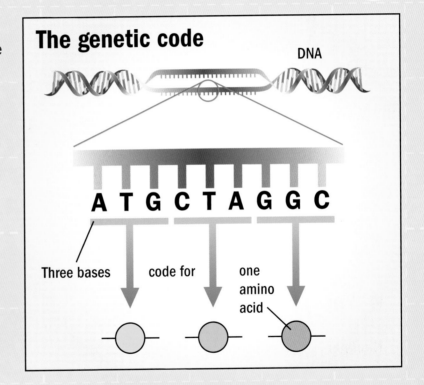

The genetic code

DNA

A T G C T A G G C

Three bases · code for · one amino acid

Breakthrough

Scientists discovered that an organism's DNA contains coded messages about how it should grow and reproduce and that RNA carries those messages out of the nucleus. Understanding this raised an interesting scientific question—could an organism's DNA be changed artificially?

Changes and mistakes in DNA

Mutation

Scientists have learned more about how DNA behaves. One important thing they have found is that changes in the DNA can happen during the life of living things (including humans).

Changes—or mutations—in the DNA inside a cell can happen for several reasons. Sometimes they take place when a cell's DNA is being copied as our body cells divide. This can cause all or part of a gene to "jump" to a different position on a chromosome. Occasionally the DNA is

Switching on DNA

In most of the different kinds of cells that make up an organism, only parts of the DNA are active, or "switched on." Various parts of DNA are also switched on at different stages in our lives. For example, some genes are switched on in the body during puberty (the time when children start to mature into adults).

Sometimes a mutation can happen in DNA that is "switched off." If this DNA is later switched on, the mutation is switched on, too.

changed when it is affected by radiation, chemicals, or **viruses**. Changes like these happen throughout our lives.

This piglet was born after the 1986 accident at the Chernobyl nuclear power plant in the Ukraine released huge amounts of radiation. This damaged the DNA among people and animals in the region, causing cancers and other illnesses. Damage to the DNA in animals' sex cells meant they often gave birth to deformed young.

Effects of mutations

Most mutations in DNA are harmless. Some can cause damage to a few cells, but have no long-term, serious effects.

Mutations in the DNA of sex cells (sperms and eggs) of adult animals show up in the young that form when these combine to make a new life. Some mutations in sex cells are harmful and result in the young having genetic disorders that mean they cannot survive or will spend their lives with an illness. Very occasionally, the mutation is beneficial (helpful or useful). This is the kind of change that can help evolution happen.

Testing, testing

People can now have tests to discover if they have faulty DNA that their children may inherit. For example, there is now a test for the gene that causes cystic fibrosis, a disease that affects the lungs and digestion, and can shorten life. Finding out that they have faulty genes means parents can make informed decisions about whether to have children. Also, in some cases, developing **embryos** can be tested for disease.

Tsar Nicholas II of Russia with his family, including his young son, Alexei, who was born with hemophilia. Hemophilia is a disease that affects the way the blood clots, making any cut or bruise dangerous. This genetic disorder appeared in the 19th century in Queen Victoria's family and spread to the Russian royal family when her granddaughter married Tsar Nicholas II.

Breakthrough

Scientists have found that our DNA can mutate or change. Some mutations can be passed on from parents to children. Scientists can now test unborn children and prospective parents for inherited mutations that are harmful and damage DNA.

Genetic modification

First steps

From the 1960s onward, scientists learned to take pieces of DNA from one organism and put them into another. By doing this, they created living things with completely new characteristics—bacteria that can make medicines, for example. This is called "**genetic modification,**" or GM.

Step 1

In the late 1950s, Professor Arthur Kornberg, from Stanford University, California, was working with DNA molecules from viruses and bacteria. He discovered an **enzyme** (a kind of protein) that can make copies of DNA segments. Other scientists discovered enzymes that could join together pieces of DNA.

Step 2

Around the same time as Kornberg was working, a Swiss scientist, Professor Werner Arber, made another discovery. He found that some enzymes from retroviruses were "biological scissors." They could be used to cut long DNA molecules into shorter sections.

"Some geniuses at Stanford University have created life in the test tube!"
President Lyndon B. Johnson, referring to the work of Kornberg and others, in an address to the Smithsonian Institution, December 14, 1967. Kornberg denied that this is what he had done.

Genetically modifying bacteria

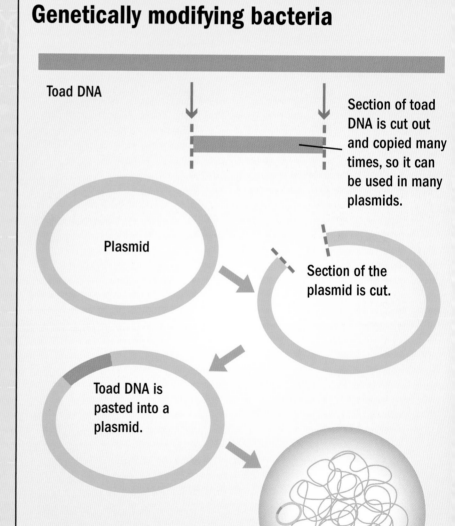

Toad DNA

Section of toad DNA is cut out and copied many times, so it can be used in many plasmids.

Plasmid

Section of the plasmid is cut.

Toad DNA is pasted into a plasmid.

Bacterium takes the plasmid, along with toad DNA, into its own DNA.

> Plasmids

Step 3

Finally, in the 1970s, the three techniques of copying, cutting, and joining were brought together by a team led by Professor Stanley Cohen, also at Stanford.

Cohen's team worked with short, circular DNA molecules called "plasmids." Plasmids are found in many bacteria. They are separate from the bacteria's main DNA. In nature, plasmids give bacteria "add-on" abilities, such as immunity to a virus or the ability to "eat" new types of food.

Cohen and his colleagues cut out a short section of DNA from a toad and then made many copies of it. They "pasted" the toad DNA into plasmids. When the genetically modified plasmids were mixed into a "culture" (growing colony) of bacteria,

This is a magnified image of a bacterium that has been treated to weaken its cell membrane, causing its DNA to be ejected. The photo shows some small loops of DNA, which are probably plasmids.

some of the bacteria took up the plasmids containing toad DNA. The GM plasmids became part of the bacteria.

"New" DNA made this way is known as "recombinant DNA"—DNA that has been "recombined."

Breakthrough

Scientists learned to cut out sections of DNA, copy them, and paste them into other organisms. This technique of genetic modification later proved useful in fields such as medical research.

GM plants

Moving on from bacteria

Teams of scientists all over the world have been working on GM plants for years. As with bacteria, it means bringing DNA from other organisms into plants. However, there are differences between making GM bacteria and GM plants.

Why modify?

GM bacteria are mostly used to produce medicines. Plants are usually genetically modified for other reasons. Some GM crops are resistant to drought or to a particular disease. Some contain toxins (poisons) that kill insect pests. Other GM crops are resistant to pesticides and weed killers, so that farmers can spray their fields without damaging their crops.

How is it done?

New DNA can be introduced into plant cells in several ways. One method is to use bacteria that infect some plants. These bacteria act by injecting their DNA into plant cells. Scientists insert a section of DNA into the bacteria, which then inject it into a plant's cells.

Another way to insert modified genes is to use a device called a "gene gun." This fires tiny particles of gold or other metal

Plants can be grown from single cells. Here, the plants being grown this way have been genetically modified. They will pass this modification on in their seeds, which will be used to grow crops of GM plants.

into plant cells. These metal particles are coated with new DNA.

Opposition

Many people oppose GM crops. They fear that GM plants may crossbreed with weeds, producing hard-to-kill "superweeds." As a result, farmers would have to use extra chemicals to keep their fields clear. This could be a threat to wildlife and possibly whole ecosystems. People worry, too, that eating GM crops could be harmful, either because they are "unnatural" or because of the chemicals used on them.

> *"Genetically modified food and crops . . . pose a serious threat to biodiversity and our own health."*
> The environmental pressure group Greenpeace

Also, GM crops grown by farmers often have infertile seeds. Farmers cannot use them to plant new crops the next year. They must buy expensive new seeds, instead. This is very unpopular, especially in the developing world.

GM crops that are resistant to herbicides can be regularly sprayed without damaging them. However, this brings with it the danger of large amounts of harmful chemicals passing into the human food chain.

Pharming

Some scientists hope to genetically modify plants and animals to produce medicines. Using plants and animals in this way has been nicknamed "Pharming." Although this has been shown to work, some people are opposed to it. They fear that plants modified to produce drugs could escape into the environment. They could contaminate other plants and the soil with harmful substances.

Breakthrough

Scientists have learned to make GM plants. Farmers can grow these as crops in the hope of increasing production and making more profit. This is still controversial.

GM animals

Modifying animals

Making genetically modified animals is a lot more complicated than making GM plants—but it can be done. These animals are described as being "transgenic." They are made by injecting "new" DNA (from another organism) into the fertilized egg of one animal and then placing the egg in the body of another—or even the same —female animal. The young she gives birth to will contain the new DNA.

Transgenic mice

The first transgenic animals were mice, developed in 1974, by Rudolf Jaenisch,

working at the Massachusetts Institute of Technology (MIT), in Massachusetts. He introduced a gene into the mice that led their offspring to develop the blood cancer leukemia.

Most transgenic animals produced since then have also been mice. Mice share 99 percent of their genes with humans, so are likely to be affected by genetic

These mice contain a gene from a jellyfish, which makes them luminous under some kinds of light. This "luminous" gene was introduced to help scientists keep track of other, more useful introduced genes.

them resistant to **parasites**. They have used DNA from sea cucumbers to genetically modify the type of mosquito that carries parasites that cause the deadly disease malaria. Scientists hope to create malaria-resistant GM mosquitoes, which will crossbreed with wild mosquitoes, making them resistant to malaria parasites, too. This could save millions of human lives.

In the tropics, mosquitoes similar to this one spread the deadly disease malaria. GM techniques used on the mosquitoes could help prevent this.

changes in similar ways to humans. They also have the advantage of being able to reproduce very quickly. However, there have been many other kinds of transgenic animals, ranging from insects to monkeys.

Why change an animal's DNA?

Transgenic animals are generally used for research. For example, researchers might make a transgenic mouse containing a human gene that they want to study. Transgenic mice can also be used to test new drugs or to try to find the genes that cause human genetic disorders. Other animals can also be used. Scientists have found that a protein made in the bodies of animals called sea cucumbers makes

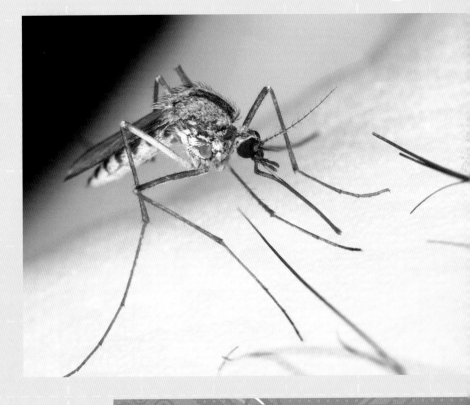

Breakthrough

Scientists created GM animals containing DNA from other living things, mainly for medical research.

Clones and cloning

Clones and cloning

Clones are individuals that have exactly the same DNA as each other. They occur naturally in bacteria when they divide, and when new plants are grown from the cuttings of other plants. Identical twins are almost clones—they develop from a single egg cell, with nearly identical DNA.

Artificial cloning

Scientists have found ways to make clones artificially. The first clones were made by splitting embryos at a very early stage, to make them produce two identical young. More recently, clones have been made by taking an egg cell from one animal, removing its nucleus and replacing this with the nucleus of a normal body cell from a second animal.

THAT'S A FACT!

Nine-banded armadillos always give birth to about four genetically identical young. They are the only mammal that does this.

The artificial cell can then develop into a clone of the second animal.

Dolly the sheep

The first mammal to be cloned in this way was a sheep named Dolly, born in 1996. Dolly was the clone of a sheep called a Finn Dorset. The nucleus of one of this sheep's cells was injected into an egg cell from another sheep. The artificial egg cell grew, was implanted in a third sheep, and was born like a normal lamb.

Since Dolly, this technique has been used to clone other animals, including cattle, cats, dogs, and monkeys.

The puppy in this picture is a clone of her mother—also shown. She has exactly the same DNA as her mother, rather than a mix of a mother's and father's DNA.

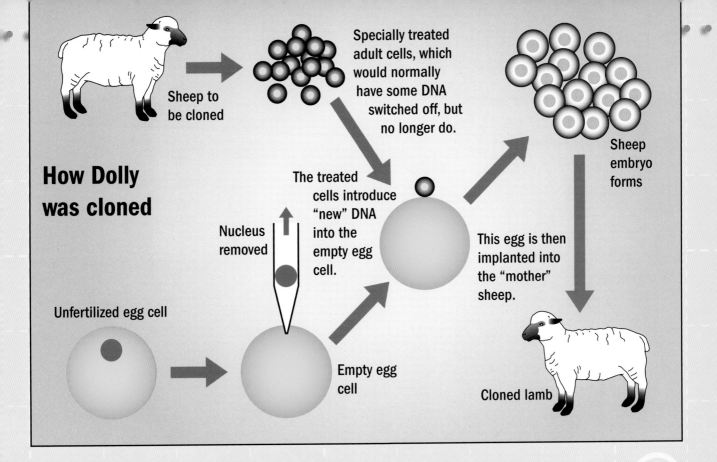

How Dolly was cloned

Sheep to be cloned

Specially treated adult cells, which would normally have some DNA switched off, but no longer do.

The treated cells introduce "new" DNA into the empty egg cell.

Nucleus removed

Unfertilized egg cell

Empty egg cell

This egg is then implanted into the "mother" sheep.

Sheep embryo forms

Cloned lamb

Cloning stem cells

Another kind of cloning could become very important in medicine. This is a technique for cloning stem cells.

Many kinds of cell, such as nerve or muscle cells, cannot divide once they are formed. These are called adult cells. However, the tissues of the body need to be able to grow and repair themselves. So each kind of tissue contains groups of special cells known as stem cells. These cells keep their ability to divide and develop.

In adult animals, stem cells can develop into only a few different kinds of cell. But very early in life, when an embryo is just a ball of cells, it contains stem cells that can turn into any kind of body cell. Scientists are very interested in these embryonic

A specially-treated adult cell from a sheep was placed in an "empty" egg. This egg was implanted into another sheep. It developed into Dolly—a clone of the original animal.

stem cells. If they could be cloned, they could be used to repair damaged body tissue, or even grow new body organs.

Embryonic stem cells usually come from embryos left over after people have had **fertility treatment**. Some people object to the use of embryos for research, saying it is destroying a life.

Breakthrough

Scientists discovered that they could genetically modify cells to produce animal clones. This led to the birth of Dolly the sheep in 1996—the first clone from an adult cell.

The ultimate map

Mapping pioneer

Work on DNA during the twentieth century was not confined to modifying, or changing it. Researchers also worked on finding out how the code is set out in unmodified organisms—including in humans. This is called "mapping genomes." (An organism's genome is its entire set of genes.)

The DNA of all living things is very similar and made up of the same chemicals. We know, for example, that human DNA is 99 percent the same as the DNA in plants!

The pioneer in this was the British scientist, Frederick Sanger. In the 1960s, he developed a way of "sequencing" or "mapping" DNA using dyes or **radioactivity** to show up each base. This was a simpler method than anything used before.

Starting small and moving on

In the 1980s, scientists used Sanger's system as they started work on finding the order in which the billions of bases in the human genome are set out. This process is called "sequencing the human genome."

The project started by mapping simpler genomes, such as those of yeasts, fruit flies, and worms. Then work started on the genome of one individual human being. The project was painstakingly slow at first. However, improved techniques and powerful computers eventually made sequencing much faster. The work involved hundreds of scientists in research centers in 16 countries. It was largely paid for by governments and charitable organizations.

Frederick Sanger

Date of birth: August 13, 1918

Place of birth: Rendcombe, England

Greatest achievement: Discovering a method—developed in the 1960s and still used today—for sequencing DNA.

Interesting fact: He won the 1958 Nobel Prize for Chemistry for work on the hormone **insulin**.

Each team worked on a different part of the genome. Work was eventually completed in 2003. Methods have now improved so much that a person's genome can be mapped in days. Scientists are still looking for ways to use the information that mapping makes available.

Who owns the genome?

The final stages of mapping the human genome were controversial. A private firm, the U.S.-based Celera Genomics, entered the race and intended to sell its findings to scientists in order to make money. Scientists working in centers that were publicly or charitably funded were opposed to this—and eventually won the argument.

"People have to take democratic responsibility for the human genome. It's not something that can be left to the commercial manufacturers, like making motor cars."

Professor Sir John Sulston of the Sanger Institute, Cambridge, England.

Breakthrough

The discovery of how to map the entire genome of every living thing, including that of humans, could lead to huge advances in medicine.

Fingerprints and profiles

A tiny difference

Everyone's DNA is 99.9 percent identical to that of everybody else. Yet that 0.1 percent difference makes each one of us unique. This is something that can be useful in many ways, including criminal investigation.

DNA "fingerprints"

In 1984, Sir Alec Jeffreys, a professor at Leicester University, England, discovered how to make clear the differences in people's DNA. He did this by copying strands of DNA until there was a big enough sample for testing. This was originally called DNA "fingerprinting"

because our fingerprints, too, are unique. It is now called DNA profiling.

Using the "fingerprints"

DNA evidence was first used in 1985, to help a young man from Ghana, who the British authorities claimed was an illegal immigrant. The man said he belonged to a family who had the right to live in Britain, and his DNA proved he was telling the truth.

A technician at the FBI National Laboratory in Boston, Massachusetts, studies a DNA profile printout. DNA from traces of hair or skin at crime scenes can be used as evidence.

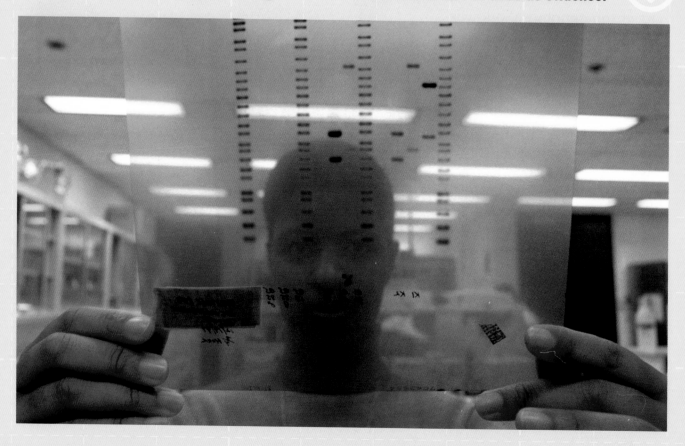

In 1987, DNA was used to convict a man named Colin Pitchfork of two murders. DNA evidence has since been used to convict many criminals. It can also be used to identify victims and even to prove that someone accused of a crime is innocent. In 1993, DNA evidence was used to get a pardon for an innocent man named Kirk Bloodsworth who was awaiting the death penalty in the United States.

DNA evidence can also help identify members of the same family. It can show whether or not a man is the father of a child, and it can help people trace where their ancestors came from.

> "My life changed on Monday morning at 9:05 A.M., September 11, 1984 . . . I realized we had genetic fingerprinting."
> Sir Alec Jeffreys

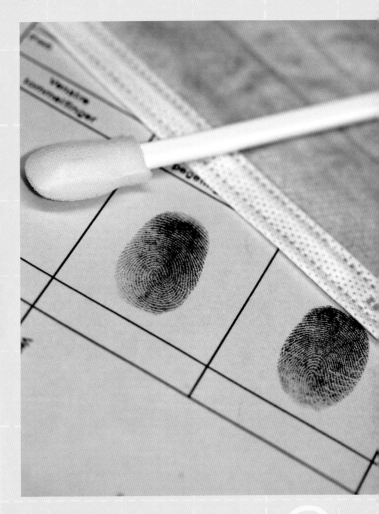

Police may now take mouth swabs, as well as fingerprints, from possible suspects, after a crime has been committed. Both are analyzed to see if they match evidence found at the crime scene.

Controversial

In Britain, the police hold databases of DNA samples from about six percent of the population, including innocent people. That figure totals about one percent in the United States, and 0.3 percent in most European countries. The British police say DNA databases help them fight crime. However, human rights activists say they are an attack on privacy and could fall into the hands of organizations that will use the information commercially. For example, health insurance companies could use the data to figure out how likely someone is to develop a disease or to die young. They also worry that these databases give the police too much power.

Breakthrough

In 1984, Sir Alec Jeffreys found a way to identify individual people's DNA. This is called DNA profiling, and it has become hugely important in fighting crime.

What next?

Using DNA

Working with and adapting DNA has already helped scientists produce better medicines and new kinds of crops. In the future, scientists will probably find many other ways to use DNA.

Gene therapy

One promising use of modified DNA is for "gene therapy." The idea is to replace faulty DNA with working DNA in people with genetic illnesses. Researchers are also looking into ways to switch off sections of DNA and stop faults from showing up.

Gene therapy is not yet safe or reliable enough for routine use in humans. One day, it may help people with all kinds of genetic conditions, including some forms of cancer and possibly AIDS.

Another possibility is "germline gene therapy." This means replacing faulty DNA right at the start of life, just as an egg is fertilized. When the egg grows into a baby, he or she will not have the genetic illness, and will not pass it on to the next generation. However, no one knows if germline therapy would work, or what the long-term effects might be. The research is also controversial because it would involve using stem cells from embryos.

Tailor-made medicines

As we understand how everyone's DNA differs, it may become possible to develop medicines that are "tailor-made" to individual needs. This would be useful because different people react differently to certain medicines—and sometimes experience nasty side effects.

Xenotransplantation

Scientists are also looking into using GM animal organs for human transplants. This is called "xenotransplantation." It could be very useful. Finding organs for transplant is difficult, as it often relies on a suitable donor dying and the person in need being ready immediately. Modified pig organs have already been used in emergencies, to keep a patient alive while a human organ is found. However, the problem of the body rejecting a transplanted organ is even greater with xenotransplantation than when using human organs.

"Genetics—science in general—produces knowledge; wisdom, how that knowledge is to be used, demands much more and may come only after long and painful experience."
Steve Jones in *The Language of Genes*

(Opposite) This GM pig in Korea was bred as part of a program to produce animals whose organs can be used in transplant surgery. Transplants now only work if the organs come from another human—and then not always. GM animals may one day provide an alternative source of organs.

Nature and nurture

Scientists are also investigating how DNA affects behavior. It seems, for example, that there may be a genetic reason why some people more easily become addicted to drugs and alcohol than others. So can we always say it's entirely their own fault if alcoholics drink and drug addicts take drugs? And, if it turns out that some kinds of criminal behavior are inherited, should this affect the way we treat the criminals?

And, lastly . . .

The more we find out about DNA, the more uses we can find for the information gained. Some potential uses are exciting and some are highly controversial, but most people agree that all future discoveries should be used for the good of all humanity. Whatever happens, one thing is certain—there will be many more breakthroughs in the remarkable story of DNA.

Glossary

amino acids chemicals containing hydrogen, carbon, and oxygen. These combine in various ways to form the proteins that make up living things.

bacteria tiny single-celled living things that can only be seen through a microscope. Many bacteria cause disease, but some can be helpful.

biodiversity the variety of different kinds of plants and animals

chromosome a tiny threadlike structure inside the nucleus of a cell that carries the genes. Each chromosome is made up of DNA inside a coating of protein.

cytoplasm the jellylike material that fills up the cells of living things

deoxyribonucleic acid (DNA) the material that carries the "code" that tells living things how to grow and develop

embryo the very first stages of a living thing. A human embryo more than three months old is called a fetus.

enzyme a protein produced in living cells that affects the way the chemicals in the living thing act

fertility treatment any treatment that enhances fertility or assists fertilization to increase the chance of pregnancy

fertilize the uniting of two sex cells—an egg and a sperm, or pollen—so that a new living thing can start to form

gene a section of DNA that influences the development of a particular characteristic, such as color

genetic modification (GM) altering the genes in a living thing in order to give it characteristics it would not normally have—for example, changing the genes of crops so that they will kill insect pests that attack them

helix a spiral or screw shape, like a twisted ladder

heredity the way the qualities and features of living things are passed on from one generation to the next in their genes

insulin a hormone (a substance that affects the way different parts of the body work) that helps the body to use sugar

mitochondria sections of DNA that live outside the cell nucleus

molecule the smallest particle of a substance, made up of two or more atoms

mutation a change in the genes of a living thing—which can often be passed on to the next generation

natural selection the way in which some individual creatures are more likely to survive and have young, depending on how well-suited they are to their natural surroundings

naturalist a person who studies nature in a scientific way, often by direct observation of animals and plants

nucleic acid a chemical found in the cells of living things—it can be DNA or RNA

nucleus the part of a cell that contains most of the genetic material, including the chromosomes, and controls how the cell behaves and grows

parasite an animal or plant that lives on or in another, and which gets its food from it—often damaging the host

pollinated when pollen is transferred to the female part of a plant to allow fertilization

pore a small hole in, for example skin, or the outer surface of a leaf

porous full of tiny holes that allow liquid, air, etc. to pass through

protein a chemical compound that is an essential part of all living things

pus a thick, white or yellowish-white fluid that builds up in infected tissue

radioactivity a feature of some elements that give out beams of subatomic particles or energy rays

selective breeding choosing the best plants or animals from which to breed in the hope that the resulting offspring will have desired qualities

trait a quality that makes something special

virus a tiny microorganism that infects animal and plant cells in order to reproduce, often causing disease

Further information

Books

America Debates Genetic DNA Testing by Elizabeth Boskey. Rosen Publishing, 2008.

Genetics by Anna Claybourne. Chelsea House, 2006.

Genetics by Lynnette Brent Sandvold. Marshall Cavendish, 2009.

The Usbsorne Internet-linked Introduction to Genes and DNA by Anna Claybourne. Usborne Publishing, 2003.

What About Genetics: From DNA to Designer Dogs by Kathleen Simpson. National Geographic Society, 2008.

Some useful web sites

Learn.Genetics™
learn.genetics.utah.edu
A great site introducing the science of genetics. It includes an interactive exercise in cloning a mouse.

DNA from the beginning
www.dnaftb.org
A clear history of work on DNA.

Basic principles of genetics
anthro.palomar.edu/mendel
About Gregor Mendel and his work on plants.

Genetics Home Reference
ghr.nlm.nih.gov/handbook/basics
More about DNA and genetics.

Kids Health
kidshealth.org/Search01.jsp
A web site that looks at some of the basics about genes and DNA. Site has areas for parents, teens, and kids.

Index